XTREME SPORTS

# ROCK CLIMBING

BY BRYAN LANGDO

EPIC

EPIC, AN IMPRINT OF BELLWETHER MEDIA BY FLUTTERBEE

# EPIC

**EPIC BOOKS** are no ordinary books. They burst with intense action, high-speed heroics, and shadows of the unknown. Are you ready for an Epic adventure?

This edition first published in 2027 by Bellwether Media, Inc.



For information regarding permission, write to Bellwether Media, Inc., Attention: Permissions Department, 3500 American Blvd W, Suite 150, Bloomington, MN 55431.

Library of Congress Cataloging-in-Publication Data is available at www.loc.gov or upon request from the publisher.

ISBN: 9798898800994 (hardcover)
ISBN: 9798898802233 (ebook)

Editor: Kieran Downs Designer: Jeffrey Kollock

Printed in the United States of America, North Mankato, MN.

# TABLE OF CONTENTS

# ON THE WALL

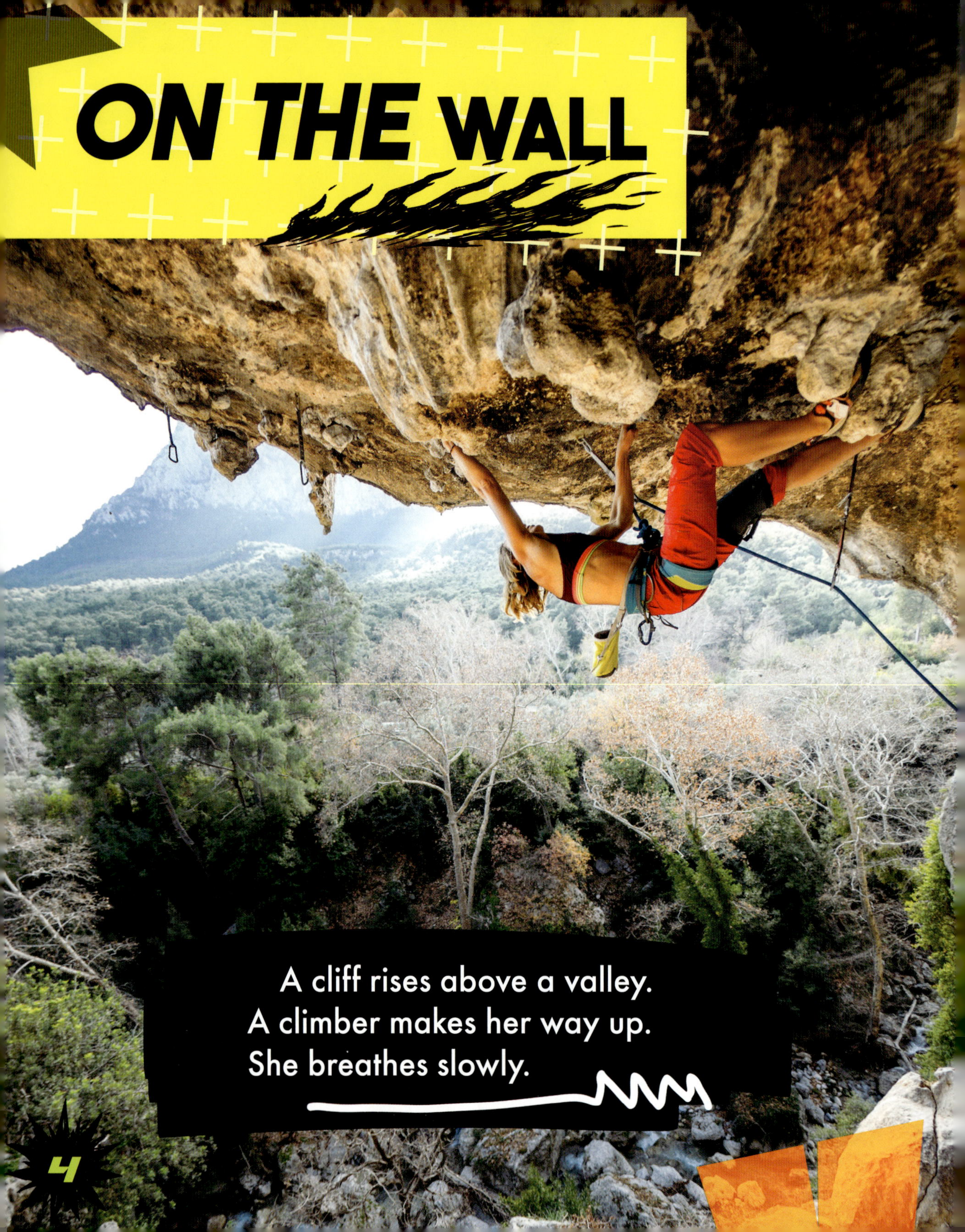

A cliff rises above a valley.
A climber makes her way up.
She breathes slowly.

Her fingers hold a thin ledge. She turns her hip and pushes herself up. This is rock climbing!

## THE FIRST CLIMB

The first known rock climb happened in France in 1492. Antoine de Ville climbed Mont Aiguille.

# WHAT IS ROCK CLIMBING?

Rock climbing is the sport of climbing rock walls. Rock climbers usually use safety ropes. Free solo climbs are done without ropes.

Bouldering climbs are less than 20 feet (6 meters) tall.

FAMOUS LOCATION

## YOSEMITE NATIONAL PARK

| LOCATION | California, United States |
| --- | --- |
| FAMOUS FOR | Having many tall rock walls and being the birthplace of modern rock climbing |

Rock climbers follow **routes**. They use **climbing grades** to tell how hard routes are.

## ROCK CLIMBING GEAR

Climbers may wear helmets. They also wear **harnesses**. Ropes hook onto them. Climbing shoes help climbers step on tiny edges. Chalk keeps their hands dry.

# THE HISTORY OF ROCK CLIMBING

mountaineering

Rock climbing was born from **mountaineering** in the late 1800s.

Climbers hammered pegs into rock walls. They hooked ropes on them. In the 1930s, Fritz Wiessner started using **anchor** bolts instead. These were safer.

anchor bolt

FRITZ WIESSNER

## A LONG CLIMB

The El Capitan Girdle Traverse is the world's longest rock climbing route. It is 14,000 feet (4,267 meters) long.

# TIMELINE

**1492** Antoine de Ville climbs Mont Aiguille

**1987** The first indoor climbing gym opens

**2007** The International Federation of Sport Climbing is created

WORLD CLIMBING

**2021** Rock climbing becomes an Olympic sport

Rock climbing became more popular in the 1960s. Climbers found new places to climb. One place was Yosemite National Park.

The first indoor climbing gym opened in 1987. It had plastic shapes for climbers to hold.

In 2007, the International Federation of Sport Climbing (IFSC) was created. It is now called World Climbing. It runs climbing events around the world.

Rock climbing was added to the **Summer Olympics** in 2021.

2017 IFSC CLIMBING WORLD CUP

2021 SUMMER OLYMPICS

FAMOUS FACE

# ALEX HONNOLD

| | |
|---|---|
| **BIRTHDAY** | August 17, 1985 |
| **HOMETOWN** | Sacramento, California |
| **FAMOUS FOR** | Completing free solo climbs of some of the world's tallest cliffs |

# ROCK CLIMBING TODAY

Climbing **competitions** take place all over the world.

## A TALL WALL

The world's tallest climbing wall is on the side of a building in Denmark. It is 262 feet (80 meters) tall!

In lead climbing events, climbers try to reach the top of a wall in one try. The higher they get, the better they score.

BOULDERING

SPEED CLIMBING

Climbers try to finish short routes in bouldering events. Whoever completes them in the fewest tries wins.

Two climbers race side by side in speed climbing events. The first to the top wins.

HOW TO

## BACK STEP

1 Get a strong hold with your hand

2 Place the outside of a foot on an edge

3 Stick your other leg out along the wall

4 Move your hip toward the wall

5 Reach for the next hold

2025 IFSC CLIMBING WORLD CUP

The world's top climbers compete at the World Climbing World Cup each year.

Many rock gyms have classes for beginners. Climbing guides take people to climb outside. Anyone can enjoy rock climbing!

# GLOSSARY

**anchor**—related to a device that holds something in place

**climbing grades**—a system of numbers that tells how hard a rock climbing route is

**competitions**—events in which someone tries to win something someone else is trying to win

**harnesses**—special belts with straps that people can hook a rope onto and hang from

**mountaineering**—a sport involving climbing up mountains

**routes**—ways for someone to climb a rock wall

**Summer Olympics**—a worldwide summer sports contest held in a different country every four years

# TO LEARN MORE

## AT THE LIBRARY

Eberth, Kristin. *Curious About Rock Climbing*. Mankato, Minn.: Amicus Learning, 2024.

Mather, Charis. *Bouldering*. Minneapolis, Minn.: Jump!, 2025.

Messner, Kate. *First Ascent: The Epic Yosemite Rock-Climbing Rivalry of Royal Robbins and Warren Harding*. Yosemite National Park, Calif.: Yosemite Conservancy, 2025.

## ON THE WEB

**FACTSURFER**

Factsurfer.com gives you a safe, fun way to find more information.

1. Go to www.factsurfer.com.
2. Enter "rock climbing" into the search box and click 🔍.
3. Select your book cover to see a list of related content.

# INDEX



The images in this book are reproduced through the courtesy of: Greg Epperson, front cover, p. 1; Jan, front cover, p. 1; Shawn Tron, front cover, p. 1; juliet_boo, front cover, p. 1; Andrey Bandurenko, p. 2; Devansphotography, p. 3; zhukovvvlad, pp. 4, 5; Basaltblick, p. 6; lzf, p. 6 (inset); Radomir Rezny, p. 7 (left); photravel_ru, p. 7 (right); Amateur007, p. 8; Александра Голубцова, p. 8 (shoes); olyphotostories, p. 8 (chalk); vitaliymateha, p. 9; Alex Photo, p. 9 (harness); Zhanna, p. 9 (helmet); Annari, p. 9 (rope); Yankovsky88, p. 10; Jones, Owen Glynne/ Wikimedia Commons, p. 10 (inset); NPGallery/ Wikimedia Commons, p. 11; Bandaneira, p. 11 (inset); Stephen, p. 11 (fun fact); Jvillafruela/ Wikimedia Commons, p. 12 (1492); sommersby, p. 12 (1987); World Climbing/ Wikimedia Commons, p. 12 (2007); Maja Hitij/ Getty Images, p. 12 (2021), 14; xartproduction, p. 13; Iain Masterton/ Alamy Stock Photo, p. 14 (inset); Christopher Michel/ Wikimedia Commons, p. 15 (left); Cavan Images/ Alamy Stock Photo, p. 15 (right); FREDERIC J. BROWN/ Getty Images, p. 15 (bottom); Xinhua News Agency/ Getty Images, p. 16; Marco Kost/ Getty Images, p. 17; Jan Hetfleisch/ Getty Images, p. 18; gubernat, p. 18 (inset); VW Pics/ Getty Images, p. 20; NAM HAE WON, p. 21; Oleggg, p. 21 (inset).